Quiet, Except for the Wind

Poems and stories from the cold desert

By Carolyn Dufurrena

Illustrations by Craig Sheppard

Quiet, Except for the Wind
Copyright @ 2016 by Carolyn Dufurrena
All rights reserved.

Writer: Carolyn Dufurrena
Illustrator: Craig Sheppard
Design/Production: C.J. Hadley

Library of Congress Cataloging-in-Publication Data
Dufurrena, Carolyn
Quiet Except for the Wind
Carolyn Dufurrena
ISBN 978-0692810347
LCCN 2016960242
No part of this book may be reproduced in any form or by any electronic or mechanical means, including information storage and retrieval systems, without written permission from the author, except by a reviewer who may quote passages in a review.

Published by Quinn River Press
P.O. Box 88, Denio, Nevada
cdufurrena@gmail.com

All rights reserved.
Copyright © 2016

$25 U.S.A.
Printed in U.S.A.

For Buster

INTRODUCTION
Diablo Meridian: The Edge of the Map

In the 1800s, great surveys marched across the West, defining the land for sale. The Salt Lake Survey grew from Temple Square in Brigham Young's capital city; the Willamette Survey marched south from Washington and Oregon; multiple surveys dithered in halting progress across California and Nevada. No consensus existed as to the location of California's northeast corner; progress east across Nevada was much like wading into a mirage. By law, no public land could be disposed of until it had been officially surveyed. A string of private contractors attempted to survey the desert, until funds ran out or snows grew too deep.

The trackless expanses offered few materials to serve as markers. Charred redwood hauled from California made section corners until there was no more redwood. Survey crews burned piles of sagebrush to charcoal and buried them with rocks to mark section corners. If charcoal corners eluded them, the survey would project the sections onto topo maps from their last position.

Today, in my neighborhood, there are holes in the map where the mark of man halts, as though at the edge of an inland sea. So in a sense, I live at the feather edge of the grid. Townships, a grid of thirty-six sections a mile square, are no such thing in this corner of the world. Elongated or cut off, some look more like narrow rectangles than anything, as though an earthquake had torn the net of man's ownership loose and it had come to rest not quite matching its former self.

A surveyor friend says, "It's just a mess. But the corners set are the corners we use, whether they're right or not." The section corners on the west side of this ranch are buried charcoal markers, the faintest trace of man's ownership before the vast blue of the endless playa absorbs all. This is where it ends, they seem to say. You're on your own from here.

In the lowermost meadow, out of sight of roads or ranch buildings, I turn a slow circle west across the valley, across the oldest fences that mark the meadow's border with the desert. Barbed wire is tacked to juniper posts mottled by orange lichen. North into Oregon, misty in the distance, east into rugged unmapped mountains: some days it feels like no humans have ever touched this place.

POETRY & PROSE

Introduction
Diablo Meridian   4

Chapter 1: Spring
Overheard in the Taylor Canyon Bar   10
Miguel, March   12
Ghost of April   13
Early Turnout to a Dry Spring   14
April Fools   15
Spring Cleaning   16
Spring Flood II   17
Family Branding   18
Bog Hot Meadow: First Pass   20
Katie in the Chicken Yard   22
Spring of a High Water Year   23
Donald Duck Cowboys With the Indians   24
Running a Trapline   26

Chapter 2: Summer
Wet Meadow Sunset   30
Barn Swallow   31
Espera, Esperanza   32
After All That   33
Between Brandings   34
From the Chimney, a Starling   35

Four Silk Shirts   36
In Cottonwood Canyon   38
Infested, Oregon   39
Kitchen Windowsill   40
Miguel, July   42
Almost Seen   43
Fire Weather Forecast   45
The Pear Tree, the Poplar, the Ditch   46
Quiet, Except for the Wind   50

Chapter 3: Fall
After the Fire I Brought Apples   56
At Texas Spring   57
In the Aspen Grove   58
Waiting For a Ride   59
October Morning   60
No Finer Tonic   61
To Cherish What Remains   62
Mantis   64

Chapter 4: Winter
The Arc of Loneliness   68
Drought in November   70
Almost Winter, 5 a.m.   71
Last Winter   71

Old Cow Dog's Winter   73
Christmas Bush   74
Blue Moon New Year's Eve   76
On Starting Colts   78
Colt-Starting Diplomacy   80
Heart of Winter   81
January, Montana   82
Pogonip   83
At Last, One Night   84
Valentine's Day   85
Waiting for the Right Wind   86
Safe Harbor   87
Winter Haiku   88
Taking Refuge   89

Chapter 5: Over the Years
Cairn: Woman Sculpted of Stones   92
Buster's Horses   94
Homeland Security: For Miguel   96
Chief   98
Wanted to Trade   100
Mapping the Landscape of the Heart   102
Miguel: Afterword   104

Acknowledgements

For my parents, who have supported me at every turn; for Linda, so generous with the beauty her eye captures; for Nancy, who read early versions of this manuscript with great critique and encouragement; for Marty, who gave me a spot to land; for Sophie's kindnesses as well as for generously contributing her father's sketches; thank you all so much. For CJ, without whom this book would not have happened. For Tim and Sam, my crew, without whose love I would not have survived the desert. Thank you all.

CHAPTER 1
SPRING

Overheard in the Taylor Canyon Bar

The bus from Idaho pulled up to the Taylor Canyon store. Brakes sighed, the door clacked open. One passenger stepped stiffly down, putting two suitcases on the gravel shoulder, shrugging into a faded canvas working man's coat. The spring wind blew cold out of the north as he picked up his bags, tucked one under a long arm, and pulled open the door to the bar, ducked his long, narrow frame through the entry.

He set the suitcases down and took a seat near the end.

"Evening," he nodded.

"Get you a beer?" asked the bartender.

"Sure. Use your phone?"

"Yep."

"I'm lookin' for work. Any ranches around here need a hand?"

The bartender wrote out some names and phone numbers on a napkin.

The first number he called, a woman answered the phone. He told her what he could do: mechanic, fix fence, drive truck. "I don't ride any more, though," he said.

They talked on a few minutes, and then we could hear the lady on the phone hesitate.

"Do you mind me asking how old you are?" We could hear her voice.

"Lady, if you have to ask me how old I am, you don't need help that bad." He hung up the phone.

I bought him a beer while he thought about things for a minute.

"Where you from, friend?" I asked him.

"Montana. Got a brother and a sister up there, both older'n me. Our parents died when we were just kids. Times were tough; we got split up when we were real young. Neighbors, other ranchers, took us in. Took us forty years to find each other."

He talked about fishing and trapping, being a hunting guide. "I used to bring folks down from Idaho to hunt coyotes here, because they said that the biggest, most beautiful pelts used to come from right here in Elko County. Story was that there were wolves here then, and they mated with the coyotes and made the biggest crossbred animal you have ever seen. Think they're all gone now. Hope so."

He rode broncs for Buffalo Bill Cody for a couple of years. "I used to reload for Annie Oakley," he said. "Reloaded those shells, put a shotgun load with a bullet on top. She couldn't possibly miss." He grinned a crooked grin. "We were engaged for a while."

"My family had a lot of pictures of that period. We gave 'em all to the Cody Museum."

He got ready to make his second phone call. I would have set there all night listening to the old man talk, but I could tell he was getting restless. He was talking to the rancher on the phone, telling him what he could do.

"Work leather, fix fence, drive truck…no more horses though."

He told him the part about the Wild West Show, and I could hear the guy on the phone pause, thinking about it for a minute. "I'll be down to get you soon as I finish my chores," the rancher said.

The tall man hung up the phone. "Do you mind if I ask you," I said, "How old you are?"

He fished a couple of dollars out of his pocket, tossed them on the bar. "I'm a hundred years old this week," he said, grinning a crooked grin from eyes bleached pale blue by the long years. "Buy these guys a round."

We nodded our thanks. He picked up his suitcases and pushed open the door. He'd wait for his ride in the dark spring wind.

Miguel, March

They say the river will run soon.
Snow is heavy in the high country:
time for Miguel to go to work.

For years, the men sharpened their shovels in the fall,
the day before they left.
In spring, they would return,
or their brothers or cousins in their place,
each knowing where the shovel waited,
in the corner of the shop.
Sling familiar, sharpened tool onto shoulder,
head out into the fields.

The meadows need Miguel.
They remember each other.

Ghost of April

Pioche motel: formica headboard,
orange velour bedspread
backed with sticky plastic;
end of a long drive, spitting rain,
from Denver.

Copper veins the ridge
behind the old mining town.
Next morning I climb
most of the way up
through sage and stunted juniper,
new boots stiff and cold
to a smooth blond ledge
in the blustery dawn.
There, a woman's fur coat,
black caracul lamb,
as though she had shrugged out of it
watching the moon
last night.
The wool curls brittle,
satin lining crumbling into dust,
its only perfume
juniper and thunderstorm.
One black velvet pump, little silver buckle,
been there maybe forty years.
I step closer.
Her feet were smaller.

I rest on the cold stone next to your coat.
It is a big valley we look across,
big and gray in the stormy spring morning.

You must have been
drunk
or crazy, or in love
to climb up here in those shoes.
It would have felt so good to take them off
in the cold limestone sand.

It's not so far from Vegas, a wild night,
a romp in the sagebrush,
the realization that you can't go back
to some drunk boyfriend
or your lockstep life
waiting for you
in that airless pink motel
a half mile down the hill.

You stood,
raised your hands to the desert sky,
dissolved
in a solution
of moonlight.

Early Turnout to a Dry Spring

All the promise of the new season withers
in sullen gray clouds that refuse to share their moisture.
We raise our eyes to the north,
scan skies for a promise of rain,
breathe in the hope of that wet desert smell—

No.
Not today.
I feel like withering too, my insides hollow.
Sweat beads my brow on cold mornings, my body
inexplicably out of tune.

Springs in the high country draw on old water deep inside;
I cross the ridge in January,
a skiff of dry snow dusting
the road I've only known in summer.

We open the gates. The calves gambol out
kicking up dust where the fuzz of green grass
should be.
I watch cattle turn back and look at me,
as if asking, "Now? Already? Are you sure?"

April Fools

Snow on the green grass.
Bright wind riffles through
puddles in the yard.

No foals in the mare bands yet,
but soon. We should move them now
from winter pasture,
but the hills are white again.
No place for them to go.
It's still winter—is it?

A flock of bluebirds flashed through
two weeks ago,
their impossible indigo a miracle of color
against the desert grays.
Cats and saddle horses
sluff a bit of winter hair,
stand shivering in a north wind.

My foolish daffodils strain
toward a rowdy sky
that will as likely crush them
under a foot of new snow tonight.

Lights on in the long shed at night,
but no lambs curl
on beds of yellow straw.
We cross our fingers,
hoping to shear before they come.

Hank shakes his head,
imagining the nightmare:
a hundred babies birthing in the chutes,
wandering lost on wobbling long legs
in the milling crowd of the shearing pens.

Five days. Maybe.
Shearers stuck in Eureka
in the snow and rain:
another one of April's little jokes.

Spring Cleaning

A high hide
in a granite notch:
avalanche of wild roses
conceals a silver pipe.
I jump hummocks in the bog,
balance on sharp boulders,
peering into the dark.
Compressor chuffing,
he hollers from below,
"See anything yet?"
Only my face
reflected in black, still water.
"Nothing yet," I say.

A thick messy braid
of roots flashes in the freezing water,
just for a moment,
like an eel thrashing back and forth.

I reach in to my shoulders and pull:
like trying to yank Ophelia
out of the depths.

She holds tight.
I lean back.
My boots teeter on
islands in the sluggish stream.
The long braid loosens,
comes all at once,
six-foot serpent of roots pulled free.

Freezing water roils high,
the earth releasing
one long, dark watery breath.

Boils, black and icy, then
clears, runs sparkling
and full,
feeding one small meadow,
the aspen grove below,
and miles down the canyon
black veins fill,
precious liquid bringing life
to the dry land.

Spring Flood II

Too tired to think, he's
up every midnight
for three weeks now,
checking the reservoir,
as though our relentless scrutiny
would keep the boulders from rolling.

Snatches a few minutes of quiet
in the afternoon,
too twitchy to sleep.

Sweeping the back porch, I pause
to gather in the sound of
river roaring under the bridge.

A brown whirlpool spins in the meadow
where the culvert should be.

The river creeps across the yard
burying the road
in rippling silver,
dangerous beauty encroaching.

Family Branding

Spring Sunday afternoon,
and all the kids are roping,
slurping lemonade between
throwing those big calves.

The oldest cousin stands,
stuffs his knife, steps away
with a word to his sister:
"Stay here and hold this calf."

It happens in a moment,
before I can turn around,
across the windy sorting lot
you're down there on your knees.

Your face a shade of gray
I've never seen on you before.
The young bay gelding shakes his head,
canters off,
his black mane flies, a victory flag
over an empty saddle.

Only a moment, twenty yards away,
but it's a while before you can stand or move.
You finish out the working day,
rope your share of calves.
Bay carries you all afternoon,
until the job is done.

Three highballs into evening,
you can barely move or speak.
Your breath comes short and careful
as you relive the day.

"I don't know what I was thinkin'
switching ropes, dropped my reins.
You'd'a caught a ration
for the stunt I pulled today.

"Saw it comin'—picked my spot,
but I still launched and
landed like a sack of, well,
that stuff that layers the corral."

Disgusted and sore,
but more than that dismayed
at the years that have betrayed you,
what you know about yourself
bucked off today
a month shy of fifty.

Bog Hot Meadow: First Pass

Silence cocoons the morning.
Snow on ridges
blue with distance,
coiling ribbon of dust
across the valley:
an invisible traveler
trundling to town.

The ticking of grass growing
marks the ripening day.

Finally,
a ripple in the wavering distance,
a russet ribbon of motion
slips in and out of view,
as though parting the silent universe
between earth and sky.

Shimmer resolves to form:
horses
moving fast across the curve of earth,
parsing the soundless space
between sage and greasewood.
Their flashing legs
dance an invisible trail
up the desert.

First Pass

They blow by thundering,
pounding the earth,
stretched full out
across the short salt grass of meadow.

Lead mare pulls up short.
She turns.
The rest swing with her.

Step. Step.
A careful trot.
Wait.

They see it.
They know what day this is.
Necks stretch low,
tails flick,
whickering
to their foals
as they decide
whether
to accept the gate,
the journey into summer.

Katie in the Chicken Yard

She would sit there all day,
balanced
on the rickety board
laid across plastic buckets
where the chickens roost;
watching the young ones peck
at their elders,
all fluffing and bawking,
cocking their cold orange eyes
at her four-year-old tallness.

Arms stretched wide, she follows them
around, around their small perimeter,
long after the egg-gathering ritual
is complete.
"Catch me a chicken, Grandma,"
she begs. "Again, again!"
She reaches,
tentative, to stroke soft feathers.
"Now, your turn."

Apprehension wars with chicken lust
in her great dark eyes.
Circling, circling, till the hen crouches,
dares her tiny sun-browned arms
to grasp that russet plumpness.
Small hands close gently.
She feels the hollow bones beneath
echo the rapid heartbeat in her chest,
the eternity, in a moment, that it takes
to master fear.

Spring of a High-Water Year

My parents come to visit,
all the detritus of difficult years
between us, between them,
hoping to clear the channel.

My father leans back in the chair,
clutches the armrests,
bracing himself against the next
conversation,
tide of dark emotion rising
high within him, a private storm
he is determined to weather alone.

I look out across the field, green with spring,
flooded with new water:
a pair of otters, the mostly unlikely creatures,
hump out of the river,
undulating joyfully across the field.
Toward the reservoir, four miles to the north?
Across the meadow, across the highway?
Into the creek...they could make it.

They do not care, their elation
that of children at the bottom of a slide,
racing to see who will be
the first to the ladder.

"Look, Dad," I said. "Otters!"
"What? There are no otters here."
I look again,
and they have passed from view.
But the current of their delight
remains with me today,
cutting a narrow path of light
in the midst of darkness.

Donald Duck Cowboys with the Indians

Those Indian cowboys had a nickname for everybody, their humor sometimes sharp, self-deprecating, often dark. This old Scandinavian buckaroo, who came to us from horse country in California, had a big nose and a loud voice, which maybe earned him the nickname from his Native American buddies.

The buckaroo gave his share of grief, but he could take it, too. He day-worked for every ranch in the country well into his seventies, broke most of the important bones in his body and had plenty of stories celebrating every foul-weather or horse-wreck day.

Ah, those McKaslands, he said. I was over at Marvin's once, cold and rainy and miserable, and there was that big Indian, talking on his cell phone. What the hell's an Indian need with a cell phone? I asked him. And he roared back and said, Too damn wet for smoke signals.

Yeah, funny as hell, but you didn't want to piss them off, that outfit. They beat that kid to death at the rodeo grounds, everybody gone, weekend of Jordan Valley, beat him with a beer bottle and then shot him.

Great to brand with, just a kick in the ass to work with, but you just don't want to get on their bad side.

Later that day, I jumped out of the truck and he was standing in the alleyway of the barn with Pistachio. We loved that buckskin filly, worked on her all winter to get her ready for the

old guy, and she was sweet. Gosh, that's a good-looking horse, I said, and then I got a little closer. His shirt was shredded, blood all over his sleeve, face all scraped up.

"Didja hear what she did to me today?" he said. "Braided her legs and fell down with me. Could I catch her? Hell, no. She just started down the road, ten steps ahead of me, all the way down. Crystal saw her coming when she topped the Wilder summit."

He headed for the bunkhouse, took a shower and a nap, and went again the next day.

Running a Trapline

One sunny afternoon in March,
just starting to be warm, he called.

"Hey, bring us beer wouldja?
We're out here on the north fence,
runnin' a trapline."

I am not in the habit
of playing cocktail waitress,
I am not the beer cart on the golf course,
but...what did you say you're doing?
It was a lovely spring day,
and I could hear something else
under that simple request,
a reason to go,
an excuse for me to be out there...
running a trapline?

I fill the small cooler, head up the road.
Choked with big sage and rye grass,
the north fence hid the cowboys
till I was almost on top of them.

Sitting on the tailgate
of the battered old truck,
hats tilted back, they were kicking their feet
like a couple of kids,
a blue plastic bucket between them.

Picking berries?
"Runnin' a trapline," he grinned.
The bucket was empty,
no foul smell of bait.
I give over the liquid sustenance.
"So, what are you trapping then?"
They are so thirsty.
"Ticks," he said,
pointing with his chin
down the fence line.

I peer under the sagebrush,
nearly seven feet tall.
Sure enough,
they'd cleared a spot in the duff:
in the center, a smoking lump. Dry ice.

"Be careful!" he said.
"They're pretty shy. Almost invisible,
but they can sure as hell see you coming."
Drawn to the mist coiling across the dirt,
coming to embrace it,
they'll freeze solid against the CO_2.

"If you scare them, they'll never come.
That bait don't last forever."

So they sit on the tailgate, swapping stories
while I skulk through the brush,
spying out their trapline real sneaky-like.
At the end, I flip over the bait.
Sure enough, the trap was sprung.

A fine fat tick as big as my thumbnail
stuck tight to the ice.
I slip him in my pouch,
(not a pouch, it's a test tube,
but that doesn't sound so poetic)
and reset the trap.

If you miss the ice,
and it's gone in thirty minutes,
the varmints will wake up and scuttle off,
waiting to leap again
on the nearest deer, or calf,
or sleeping cowboy.
Timing is everything,
when you're hunting ticks.

*For the last several years, we have been
helping a group of research scientists
develop a vaccine against a deadly
tick-borne disease that causes cattle to
abort their calves just before they're due.
We had to determine the presence of the
tick before we could qualify for the CDC's
live vaccine trial, so these buckaroos were
actually conducting pretty important
research that spring afternoon.*

CHAPTER 2
SUMMER

Wet Meadow Sunset

The first pair of cranes
stand tall as people
talking, talking to the geese,
warning the ducks
which perhaps have not noticed me
or the black and white marauders,
my constant companions,
slipping along the willows
at the edge of their world.
They stand sentinel a long time
as I edge around them,
sunset firing up a sheet of blue water,
skimming the salt grass meadow
crowded with avocets, killdeer,
curlew, ibis. Herons stalk,
picking morsels
from the banquet.
A moveable feast landed here
just this moment,
this wet spring evening
in the desert.

Barn Swallow

Caught by one foot in a tangle of twine
up under the bunkhouse eves.
He struggles and flutters
but cannot free himself.
Heart of safety and warmth
become a death sentence.
I climb onto the old red chair,
reach up.

He flattens himself into the nest.
Fingernails gather
rough string, mud, fledgling
all together,
tight against my chest.

One hand fumbles for small scissors…
kitchen shears will have to do.
Awkward, snipping at the
great fiber puzzle
around tiny bones grown into the snarl,
claws withered, toes tortured together.

Tail feathers ragged: can you perch
with one good leg
on that wire with your brothers?
My giant fingers work the panicked creature
toward his brief freedom.

He contemplates me, still as death
in the palm of my warm hand.
The last of the trap falls to the floor.
On the porch in the bright morning,
he hears his fellows cheering, sees them
swoop and glide.
My hand opens.
Small strong wings rocket him up
into the blue,
the joyous song: it doesn't matter
if I make the winter.
I have known what it is to fly,
the ecstasy of freedom.

Espera, Esperanza

Esperanza,
the word for hope,
sound of softly running water.

Inside it, espera,
the word for wait. The old man looks off
across the meadow,
across the years:

"I remember seven years together
when the water did not run."
Espera,
esperanza.
Wait for the water,
wait and hope.

Perhaps faith
is the echo that is left
when the memory of heaven
fades.

After All That

I forgot the
hard-boiled eggs.
They should be here,
peeled with weathered hands
under sweaty hats
as the boys shade up under the trailer
after branding.
Dust-clogged throats cooled and cleared with cheap beer
liberally laced with Clamato juice,
a rain of salt and red Tabasco.
Thirty miles up the country
they watch three hundred head of cattle
feed off north into the heat of afternoon.

Stomachs growling,
they'll make do, once again
with what they have.

Between Brandings

Ibuprofen and Early Times,
a frozen slab of home-cured bacon
wrapped in a clean white T-shirt
tucked in the hollow of your back
dulls the knife wedged
between your lumbar vertebrae.

Not like cortisone,
not like surgery:
not going to town for a while.

From the Chimney, a Starling

Just a thump, and there he is:
flat on his back,
leathery feet in the air,
upside down
amongst the half-folded laundry.
I come closer.
He blinks,
as though coming back from the dead, staring at trees
which should have been so accessible,
and yet held away from him by the
bright window glass;
blinked again
as my hand closes over him,
shocking him back
to consciousness.
I open the back door,
then my palm.
He leaps into the terrifying freedom
of the cold morning.

Four Silk Shirts, 1955

She raised four kids on a lonely place
on the edge of the Black Rock Desert.
They lived on what they could raise or shoot,
ninety gravel miles from town.

She patched their jeans and mended
torn leather, reworked their duds
again and again,
hoping for new things one day.

She slept on an iron bed in the corn
when the ears came close to ripen.
Her rifle slept beside her
underneath the summer moon.
She laughed. The deer heard
the bedstead squeak,
and gave her plenty of room.

The bomber comes low and fast that day,
practicing for war.
Whizzing shells whack against the barn.

The pilot's eyes widen
at the children in the yard,
the young woman in the garden.
He's not much older than the boys,
she thinks, and wonders just where
they might be, down the desert
gathering strays.
Another day she hears him come,
further off this time
looks up to see a mass of white,
fluttering to the ground.

She catches up the sorrel mare,
trots out to investigate,
a sheet of silk is captured there,
billowing in the breeze.
She hobbles Sorrely some distance off
to save the long walk home.

Picking the fabric free of thorns,
She sees it's tattered, but not worn.

She rolls it tight,
ties it on, turns for home.

Heading back across the flat,
colors come to mind:
mint green, sky blue, sun's yellow gold,
as it lights the baby's ear:
bright, soft pink as she's laughing there.

That night she cuts out four silk shirts.
It's almost time for Fair;
mint green, sky blue, sun's yellow gold,
bright pink of the baby's ear.
Beautiful, but tough and sleek,
they won't tear on barb wire fence:
a second skin for her children
who ride far and free and beyond her reach
most days across this rough country.

Decades later, one of her sons said:
   "Those boys did shoot up the shop, sometimes, and we'd find live fifty-caliber shells while we were riding out there on the desert. Once we found a whole clip. I guess that was pretty dangerous, us kids riding around out there with unexploded ordnance in our saddlebags.
   "There wouldn't have been parachutes unless there were dead guys. And there were dead guys, a couple, in a plane wreck. The helo brought two of them into the ranch to meet the ground transport.... Yeah, I remember those shirts. I was seven or eight, but I think it was the target they were pulling that she made those shirts out of, not the parachutes. The Navy would have picked up parachutes. Later on, we were racing some of those two- or three-year-old colts. John was timing 'em and one ran through the barbwire fence with him. He got cut up, but he would have been cut up a lot worse if he hadn't'a been wearing that shirt."

In Cottonwood Canyon

Riding the creek, dry in the drought,
he hears something snap
under the big gelding's hoof:
a long black PVC snake hides in the brush,
and over there, another, all these long miles
out in this desert canyon.
He follows the slithering pipe
up the canyon, a quarter mile
to the source: the big trough, where
many cattle water, every other year.
Someone's grow patch,
its crop long harvested.
He scans the ridges anyway:
lotta rocks to hide behind,
if you're guarding the treasure
that was here.

Infested, Oregon

Summer morning,
hot with dust,
heady with the smell of pine.
White butterflies cloud the air:
the air vibrates with them.
I can hear them chewing through the needles
as they consume
the forest.

They cover every bush,
scatter on my shoulders,
flitter through the trees
like snow
that does not fall.

Kitchen Windowsill

Lace curtains frame the window
where I sit.
On the sill, a ranch house altar
to works of God and man we come across
in the course of a summer's day.

The clump-ching of boots recedes
with the raucous talk of men.
Silence swirls; the house breathes deep.

Crystal fragment, mammoth knee,
volcanic cobble of air-pocked glass,
bubbled rind of copper picked
with a fingernail off a smelter wall
in another life.

Robin's nest, a young son's gift,
rough with straw and baling twine outside,
smooth as pottery within.
Holds half a blue eggshell.

Iron-stained bottle
my love found buckarooing,
iridescent sheen over bubbled glass,
crusted with candle wax
from when the power went out
Mother's Day.

Tufa-cemented handful of pebbles
from an ancient lakeshore.
A tiny spider lives inside:
arachnid cathedral,
shaded from the sun.

My favorite: a cobble, smooth as silk
polished in the belly
of a dinosaur,
an easy morsel carried
across miles of swamp,
across millions of years,
roiled and smoothed and come to rest

Big boys,
learning to read
October to March,
between harvest and planting
between shipping and turnout:
boys doing the work of men.
Warm stone smooth in my palm,
I dislodge silken spider strands:
it must be time to clean.
I see again the givers of these gifts,
the tellers of the tales:
stories of flesh that draped bone,
man who drank whiskey, boy
who climbed trees:
messengers from another time,
floating out there
waiting to be seen.

inside the arc of a giant ribcage
mired in silt. A teacher's gift,
from white-haired Margaret,
schoolmarm on the Black Rock
when one-room school meant
eighth-grade boys with full beards,
as old as she, or older.

Miguel, July

Breeze blows across the meadow
deep in rye grass, bluestem, fescue.
An ocean of softness bending to the wind's touch
across all things standing still.

The waving grass conceals his journey
across the field
as he changes water,
the tiny figure wading to his shoulders in meadow hay.

He surfaces,
the flash of his shovel blade
like a fish jumping
in a green sea.

Almost Seen

One full-moon night in August
two sandhill cranes flew
over the house
into the Payne Field.
Their haunting cries in the purpling dusk
stopped me in my tracks.
I ran out into the white gravel road,
hoping for a glimpse
of them in moonlight
through tall cottonwoods
that blocked the sky.

Fire Weather Forecast

Sun tops the trees through a red-tinged smudge.
Dawn's a breathless ninety-five degrees.
All summer long that East Pacific High
presses
on our valleys,
keeps the rain away.

Thunderstorms scatter heat lightning
like mean schoolboys
across crackling dry foothills
that only days ago
were deep in green grass,
fragrant
with wild roses.

Heat lightning flickers,
dishes rattle in the cupboard.
Dogs pant in the hot shade.
Tempers spark with the heat.
I suck ice under the fan,
wait for a change
in the fire weather forecast.

The Pear Tree, the Poplar, the Ditch

A family of red-tailed hawks patrols the old orchard, home to an underground city of badgers, ground squirrels and chipmunks. Hawks share the small mammals with a family of great horned owls living in the abandoned barn. They hunt the line of silver poplars that mark the border of the ditch.

"That poplar tree split right down the middle," the old man says, "during the windstorm the other day." He doesn't walk over there to look. The uneven ground of the orchard is too treacherous for him now. He doesn't trust his legs, or his balance, to carry him over broken ground in a place where the kids might not think to look for him if he falls.

When he was a boy living on the little ranch at the foot of the canyon, he'd gather the orchard's winter pears. "As big as your hand," he says, holding out a massive palm that could hide a grapefruit. He and his brother brought them by the bushel, for his mother to wrap, one at a time in newspapers, to rest in the cool cellar, carefully kept from bruising. All through his growing-up time during the long years of the Depression, the pears appeared on the table Christmas morning, filling the sparkling glass bowl, green and crunchy sweet.

For three decades after the little ranch was sold, it was a seasonal buckaroo camp, home to cowboys from May to the first of September. People from the big corporate outfit that absorbed the place kept the orchard irrigated.

The trees gave up their fruit to whoever came by: cowboys, ranch cooks, hunters, deer, folks from town who knew about the twenty-odd trees that had been planted there at the base of the mountain so long ago. The oldest apple trees were mature in 1905.

"When they grubbed out the sagebrush to make the hay meadow," the old man says, "those apple trees were there then." The old-timers knew when the cherries would be ripe, plums in late July, pears in August.

The big outfit changed hands more than once, and when the headgate washed out sometime in the 1980s, the new folks didn't fix it. It was thirty-five miles up the valley from headquarters. Nobody lived at the little place anymore. Cowboys hauled their horses back and forth to the main place, rather than live in the little line camp. The new people had no interest in the fruit trees, and no knowledge of the orchard's larger role in the valley as the source of cherry pies and apple cobblers for neighbors who had no fresh fruit of their own.

For two or three years, those trees went without water from the ditch. Most of the old orchard died, except for the winter pear tree. Even in drought, it still gave a few pears.

The ranch sold again. The new owner called the old man and asked him about the ditch. He would pay to fix it if somebody knew how to get it done. So the old man hired a backhoe, hired a guy to dig the ditch out and replace the big headgate that brought water to the hay meadow, the houses and the orchard.

"Better get up there and change the water in the orchard," he'd tell his son, who was managing the big outfit by then. Seventy miles round-trip once or twice a week wasn't that much for folks used to the vast spaces of this empty country. The pear tree came back right away, sheltered by poplars from the desert winds. After a couple years, they would find the tracks of pickups that had parked under the tree in August, where someone had been gathering a few pears. Deer bedded down nearby, and their tracks were under the pear tree too.

The Ditch
"Watch for snakes," he says, as I tip the shovel onto my shoulder and set off into the head-high sagebrush to change the water. "Take a dog with you." Three dogs leap into the bed of the truck, two young border collies and one obstreperous old gray mutt, whose selective deafness and urge to travel has nearly cost him his life more than once. Shaggy and long-haired, he looks and runs like a wild cousin of the Hound of the Baskervilles. He will disappear moments after the tailgate drops, not to be called back until the moment he hears the engine crank for the trip home.

The dogs do their job, alerting any sleeping reptiles of human progress through the sagebrush. The hillside above the little ranch is mostly chunks of black basalt sunk in coarse sand and alkali mud. Changing the water where the creek is narrow is an easy task—a few shovelfuls of sod and a big rock or two and the water shifts to irrigate either the hay meadow to the north or the orchard. Still, timing is important. Twelve hours after the soil is saturated, the flow spreads out through the sagebrush, drowning the small channel and the grasses between, turning the sandy slope into a boggy morass.

Uphill the channel is deeper. The stream wends its quiet way down between pocked volcanic boulders and red lava. Shoveling chunks of sod, jumping from one side to the other in search of likely rocks to secure them, it is easy to lose oneself in the daily task, soaking up the breeze, the rushing sound of water, the one small moment when the current shifts into the south-trending channel, racing downstream to soak the fruit trees and the dry meadow below.

"The ditch was dug sometime soon after the Civil War," the old man says. Every canyon had prospectors and homesteaders, and there was a little settlement, just a collection of miners' dugouts, near the head of the canyon. They tried to build a ditch from there to bring the water out, but the grade was too steep, the ground too porous, water leaking through the granite sand.

"I worked that ditch more than once," he said, "when I was young." He tore out weeds and shoveled willows that clogged the channel, the better part of three miles in length. He threw big rocks out of the channel and lined it with fine-grained dirt hauled from nearby meadows. He and his father moved the headgate to a more likely spot downstream.

They changed the path the ditch would take, leveling it with a kitchen chair, the uphill legs sawed off short. A glass of water on the seat told them if the homespun engineers' path was plumb. Eventually they got it right, and water would stay in the ditch most years, roaring down from high snowpack into the orchard. The ditch watered those twenty-odd fruit trees in the foothills for the better part of forty years.

The Poplar
The windstorm split the poplar tree fifteen feet above the ground. The whole great mass of it came down at once, cracking in half all along its considerable length. The tree was mostly dead, standing long after the bark had peeled, suckers persisting along one side.

Its silver trunk stretches a hundred fifty feet into the grassy orchard, a meadow open to the sun now that most fruit trees are gone. The poplar looks somehow peaceful, at rest now

after years and years of holding back the winter storms, guarding the orchard and the whitewashed stone bunkhouse, the barn and cookhouse. Its upper branches must have hit the winter pear tree, or maybe it was the wind, bringing the smaller of its two main trunks to earth as well.

Water meanders along the ditch between century-old poplars, moistening the late-summer meadow and the winter pear tree. A second row of young trees has volunteered behind the grandfathers, and someone has diverted the water in the ditch to feed them. The young poplars are perhaps three feet in diameter at the base, strong and straight, growing up to take their place as the guardians of the orchard, as long as the water flows. The old tree's partners stand sentinel still, creaking in the smoky south wind of autumn.

Every August my husband and I throw the long-handled fruit picker into the truck with a handful of paper sacks and cardboard boxes. "Time to go get those pears," the old man says. We'll bring him the best ones, and he'll hold them in his calloused hands, and look off north for a minute, and ask us, did we turn the water?

Quiet, Except for the Wind

The phone call came about three o'clock, a Sunday afternoon in August. Lightning had struck in a brush-choked canyon thirty miles from ranch headquarters, where a complicated mass of inaccessible terrain falls away to the Columbia Plateau to the north and rises south to the mountains and valleys of the basin and range. Deep, steep-sided canyons climb to granite ridges fringed with head-high bitterbrush and sage. North and south, east and west are a jumble of topography.

Feed was thick that year, but brittle, dry. The year before had been as bountiful in moisture as this year had been austere; fire would run hot through that dry brush and bunch grass. For a while it looked like we would get through the summer all right. It had been a long time since the last fire in these mountains; it was our turn.

At first, it seemed like there were opportunities to stop it. The bottom of Cottonwood Canyon the first day, the top of Maggie Creek summit the second afternoon. There were windows of time, after the first gather brought the cattle off Holloway Mountain, ash raining on the cowboys' hats, when it looked like the fire would settle. "We had to leave a cow with a day-old calf. They just couldn't make it over the summit," said Crystal, one of our buckaroos. "But there's a spring there; she could have gone back to that green spot with him." You could tell she was trying to keep that image in her head.

The cowboys ride back in the next day to gather Maggie Creek, pushing cows and calves westward down to the flat, ahead of the plume that grows by the hour. Herds inevitably get mixed up in the high country, but there isn't time to sort the neighbor's stock, and those pairs travel down the canyon into unfamiliar terrain. They don't like to be in strange country, and by evening a dozen of them head back up the same canyon with their calves, trying to get home on trails that are burning.

Fires in Nevada usually blow up and burn fast, done in three days. This fire eats a canyon a day, day after day, blowing north into Oregon, east into the next valley, then back west. Five days in, and by this time there is a Type Two Incident Management Team camped out around the local two-room school. The fire creeps south along the ridge all day Friday, until the wind kicks up. Firefighters are already spread thin when another lightning strike over east of us causes fire managers in town to pull all the airplanes to another fire. The wind is blowing twenty-five miles an hour.

I am on my way home from town when Tim

sheepherders, and enough horses to do the work come and go from May through October camping out in this small corner of paradise. Although the camp is hidden in an aspen-fringed draw, the kids riding up there could probably see smoke from the ridge.

The fire is still fifteen miles away. There should be more than enough time, a couple days maybe, to gather and move the cattle from the high valley; move the herders, get the band of sheep to safer pasture.

"Don't come up here," he says.

"I won't," I promise. Still, I drive the highway north on past headquarters, watching the billowing plume of smoke. The fireline has been creeping its way south along the ridge, but in what seems like a moment, in that hour before sunset when the summer winds blow hardest, it flashes into life. Mud Creek, Shyster Creek, Sage Hen: in minutes the fire eats into fifteen miles of ridgeline. I watch it approach the twin peaks that mark the horizon just above sheep camp. I call Tim.

"Where are you?"

"We're getting the hell out of here," he says. His brothers and the kids are ahead of him horseback. The herders are waiting on the road someplace ahead, camp packed, dogs nervous. My sister-in-law is driving another truck ahead of him, with everything from the house they could gather. He's in the drag, the last one out.

calls me. "I'm going up to camp to help get the horses out. I might stay up there tonight." Camp is a forty-acre pasture, a cabin and an outdoor kitchen tucked under a grove of aspens by a little spring. It makes for a cool getaway from the heat of summer, a rustic mountaintop base of operations. A handful of buckaroos, a couple of

"There's fire on three sides of us. We're getting the hell out," he says again.

"What about the sheep?" I ask.

"Wait for me at the hot springs," he says.

"I love you," I say. But he is already gone.

Crystal is waiting at the ranch house. "Come get me," she says when I call her. I turn my truck around and go back to pick her up. We drive faster than anybody should back to the hot springs.

"Oh Jeez," she says, when she sees the glow lighting up the ridge. "Oh Jeez." It's dark by now. We are just waiting, watching for headlights.

Normally it takes a couple of hours to trail horses out of camp. The horse trail runs down a rocky road from the cabin, up over a ridge, down the other side, through another canyon. Tonight, they don't have that kind of time.

It's quiet, except for the wind. We walk back and forth in the tumbleweeds. My flip-flops crunch in the gravel. Stupid, not to have changed into boots and jeans before. The glow brightens. The fire crew is camped somewhere nearby, but they seem to only work the day shift, and this fire is working all night.

My eyes bore holes into the darkness looking for headlights. His life is not supposed to end tonight, I think. Not this night. Not this way. Crystal's phone rings.

"Where are you?"

"Bring the horse trailer to the Texas Spring Corrals," he says.

And so we bring the horse trailer, making our way through the moonless night, cows and calves running every which way, scattered across the crested wheat field in the dark. At last, headlights appear. They're out of the canyon. We pull up the hill, and our lights show us seven horses, heads hung low, seven cowboys—all family—leaning on their necks. Sheepherders, dogs, all exhausted, but accounted for.

Halters are passed from hand to hand. Horses thump into the big trailer, cowboys talking low and gentle to the animals that have brought them all out safely.

"What about the sheep?" I breathe, asking Tim in the dark. A thousand head, one of two bands, are in a corral on top of a high ridge. Left loose, they would surely run before the fire, and the hope is that with the short brush on top, that there are enough of them, the ones in the middle might survive. He looks up the ridge. "The fire has passed them. They're already burned over." The trucks head out. They have done all they can for this night. It's ten-thirty p.m.

Early the next smoky morning, the fire burning slower in the relative coolness of the August morning, we must go back up and find the corral where the sheep have spent the night. The truck creeps over the rough road, a hopeless silence fogging the cab. Patches of brush are still burning. A fawn lies on a smoking hillside where it has collapsed, overtaken by racing flames in the night, its feet and ankles burnt black.

The truck groans over the last hill to the barren saddle where the sheep corral waits. Somehow, this band has survived the night, although the ewes on the outside are singed. Some will die later, their lungs white with ash, but for now the herders, shaking their heads, open the wire gate and gently guide the animals off toward the blackened canyon where they can make their way to the low country in relative safety.

The other band is trapped on a high peak in the north, surrounded by fire on all sides. The two herders have put their sheep on the rugged summit where no grass grows, and it has kept them safe, if isolated, for the last two days. The men are up at dawn, beating the creeping fire with their jackets to make a wide circle of safety around their animals. It has been working, but they must get them to water soon. They wait two days for the fire to pass the part of the canyon where there is a good stream of water. At last they are able to reach the spring, but there is still too much fire in the lower reaches to risk trying to trail them out. So they sit there, watching the flames eat one canyon after another as the wind changes, watching the firefighters like ants, moving far below. They drink from the spring, keep their animals quiet, watch and wait. It will be two more days before they can bring them down.

The fire will burn south for a fortnight, racing down the ridges, eating its way down the slopes like lava flowing in the night, but fast, faster than any lava flow. The firefighters cannot get ahead of it. In the end, it will be 720 square miles of blackened earth.

CHAPTER 3
FALL

After the Fire, I Brought Apples

After the fire, I brought apples from the orchard, boxes of them, loaded on the floor of my old Ford. I took them up the blackened canyon to the spring, a tiny island of green, scorched at the edges. One yearling doe, shell-shocked and singed, stood hunched, unable to move. I threw her a handful of apples. She did not sniff them. She watched me, disoriented, wobbling a little.

I kept on up the canyon, looking for something to show me that life was still possible. The meadow at the head of the canyon was black. Upland grasses, iris, penstemon and millions of little yellow wildflowers were gone, burnt to a sooty dusting over the sparkling granite sand. I threw apples out here, there. I saw no animals but I thought perhaps they would come later.

The road plunges over the ridge down a steep hill into aspen groves, which fill swales between hummocks and spires of granite. The fire ran hot through here, but some south-facing slopes have been spared. The north slopes are all bare, everything torched to ash.

Half a dozen does with their fawns are startled by my passage up the hill. I toss more fruit. They are mountain creatures: how would they know what these round offerings are? I empty my box, drive to the cabin, sit on the porch in the bright sunshine. It's cool here now, even though September is a week away. I sit and stare, as shell-shocked as these deer.

After a while, I climb back into my truck and drive down the hill. Pink plastic flagging tied on the remains of sagebrush by the fire crew waves cheerfully against the black, fluttering a bright message without meaning. Fawns lie dead; their tiny feet could not carry the small bodies further. There must be solace at the end of this day, I think, and then I see them.

At Texas Spring

Stripped bare.
Angular bones of the mountain
lie charred; soot drifts in
the rocky canyon,
still and hot in late summer sun.

Suddenly, a cloud of alkali bursts to life,
fluttering indigo, turquoise, sky blue flashing
at its heart.
Two bluebirds
taking a dust bath
between the blackened boulders:
dancing in the heart of destruction.

They explode skyward
washed clean,
free.

In the Aspen Grove

Saplings spring up
between their
blackened brothers.
October's cooling,
frost no object.
Some trees, barely left alive,
leaves blanched to ash,
suddenly sprout new green just weeks before frost,
the grove desperately holding on,
determined
to live.

Waiting for a Ride

They pile off the bus at the end of the road, that plume of white
coming fast across the valley. Five minutes.
The bus door creaks shut, the brakes hiss.

"What about your lunch?
You know you didn't eat it.
You're gonna be in trouble."

He pops the clasp on the metal box.
"Stupid corn dogs," he says,
grinning into the brush.
Yep, there they are.
He snags the wooden stick,
flips the rejected meal
onto a small dirt mound.
Dark eyes measure him,
evaluate the risk.

In a flash,
the kit fox leaps,
drags the greasy prey into its lair,
victorious.
The pups will feast
again tonight.

October Morning

A sprinkle of rain just before dawn:
I bring the dogs in,
watch gray light define insinuations of deer,
silent, graceful,
drawn into the yards by apples,
buckets of them,
strewn in the lee of the long shed:
three antlered bucks, two dozen does, their fawns—one black.
The old cut-eared doe no longer stands on ceremony,
flumps down under the eaves in the train of apples,
working her old jaw
in sweet ecstasy.

No Finer Tonic

The smell of October dawn,
horses, leather, sage and last night's rain.
The swell of the Divide,
granite, mahogany-wedged crags,
distant King Lear purple in the dawn.
This is why I came here,
and this is why I stay.

To Cherish What Remains

Trunks black or strangely reddened,
some not burnt at all,
weeping sap near the ground, as though aching for their compatriots in flames.
Others, golden fall leaves quivering, bursting clusters of new buds,
nickel-sized green leaves among the gold,
the grove confused by all that's happened.
Is it spring? Fall?
Are we alive?

Baby aspen sprout thick under the burnt canopy, save on the north slopes,
where the fire ran hottest;
there, only mica sparkles through the soot.
High in the granite of the Rock Fort, the rugged outcrop where the children
used to play, a massive nest is burnt to cinders, revealing packrat treasures:
old drawer handles, tin foil, rusted hinges:
ancient treasures, cached up high,
safe from most danger,
but not from all.

Some logs are burnt to ash, but inches away
piles of deadwood are left unsinged.
The old shoeing corral has disappeared,
but the slash pile next to it remains untouched.

Great old aspens, marked with the passing of sheepherders
a century ago, stand tall, their trunks thick,
burnt clear through at the base.
One topples, others stand.

For now.
Some of the south slopes survived, protected by the ridge.
Sometimes. The wind is fickle in these canyons.

The trees that fall this winter will make lumber for new corrals.
The old outhouses are burnt to ash, and that is a good thing,
grass has already started some places, and it will come back with the snow.
Rebuild the fence, rebuild the corrals. Start fresh with the spring.
Be ready when the mountain is, to accept the animals again.

Mantis

Mantis: August

The sun crawls red-orange through the smoke, a chilly north breeze after a long hot night. The geraniums are starting to bloom again, as the sun moves south at dawn.

The narrow, sand-colored mantis starts at my stride across the grass. She recognizes the threat, and runs. She does not fly. She is big, big enough that I can see her easily, in sharp contrast to the bright lawn. She sprints in two spurts: across the grass, a pause, then up the elm tree. She climbs just high enough to be out of reach, and turns, watching me, sending me her little death message.

Mantis egg-laying time: Denio School

The little boys brought her in from the tumbleweeds that were starting to blow on the playground. Cold at night, it would freeze any day now. She seemed content to rest in the terrarium, calling silently to the crickets the little boys brought in. The boys stood, transfixed, as the crickets stepped closer to her, mesmerized by some inaudible sound, some chemical trance. She stared at them, motionless, until with blinding speed she snapped the heads off each one, crickets, grasshoppers, seemingly whatever species they deposited in her realm.

She lay her eggs in a hard walnut-sized case on the ceiling of her prison, warm near the small light, and seemed content to wait, her patient predatory nature taking on all comers until the little boys ran out of crickets and the grasshoppers all froze. Then they brought in a platoon of carpenter ants. She did not try to eat the ants. They seemed impervious to her song. They swarmed over her, the six or eight of them, a few at a time. She could only fight most of them, and one chewed a hole in the back of her leg. The next morning she was dead.

The heartless children squealed in awe, in the name of elementary science. Tiny

Mengeles. Nature at every level is harsh, heartless, extreme. Nature is no gentle deity. It is a monstrous force, in which alpha becomes prey in a heartbeat.

I am left with a poignant affection for the mantis. I dump the terrarium soon after in the school yard, which is when I find the egg case, tucked discreetly inside the roof. I store the terrarium behind a pile of boxes in the back room with the water heater and the brooms, hoping the janitor will not notice, but she does. She moves it to the leaky shed, where next spring's mantis babies might have a fighting chance come spring.

The Corn-Row Mantis

I am tearing out corn stalks at the back of the garden, late September by the fence. This mantis is lime-green, invisible against the slender inner leaves of corn plants. She is bright against the railroad tie she has chosen for her egg case. I watch, transfixed, as she works and works, extruding a mass of foam layer by layer. Many times larger than her body mass, it will harden soon.

I move away awhile, work in another part of the garden, and come back to see her progress. She labors still, more slowly now. At last she finishes and sits, exhausted, on the tie, watching me demolish the last of her forest. I pick her off her perch and settle her in the late corn, which will stand another week or two, but it feels futile, after-the-fact. She lets me move her into cover, but the sense of finality in her slow movements brings me again face to face with the same feeling, a patient waiting for the end of all things.

CHAPTER 4
WINTER

The Arc of Loneliness

A continuum runs from solitude to agony, from contentment to gentle ache to thrumming craziness, where you stand at the grocery checkout counter, unable to stop talking to the clerk even after the bags are filled and the receipt handed over, realizing finally with the exasperated sigh of the woman behind you that you are just filling your heart with this conversation, because it's the last conversation you will have with a woman, for weeks.

Drought in November

After dark
I hauled the hose
out of the shed,
sprayed water
into the flower beds,
packed with raked leaves
against the winter.

I pretended
it was rain
ticking onto
the brittle chips,
softening them
into the earth.

Almost Winter, 5 a.m.

Spiderweb bellying in the cold November breeze,
wind chime's tinkling becomes more urgent.
Cold brilliance of winter stars arcs over
the blue dark of morning.
I hurry through downed drifts of dying summer
to yellow kitchen's warmth.
Flies still circle in southside windows,
around and around,
hiding from the coming chill,
the long winter's sleep
awaiting them.

Last Winter

…was really bad, she said.
So dark, so cold,
so long and boring on the plains.
Enslaved by inertia,
by the exhaustion of fighting
him for every inch of freedom.
No wonder
the chained dog
at last lies down
and dies.

© LINDA DUFURRENA

Old Cow Dog's Winter

I. November 30th

Steady rain soaks the morning,
gray curtain all but hiding nearer hills.
Red hen forsakes her nest
across the yard, scolds old Cookie
to make room in that doghouse.
Two male robins
preen foolishly in the yard
for mates long gone south.
Sick fawn shows herself
at noon: laggards of the season,
given a reprieve
that ends today.

II. First Snow

Skiff of white across dry grass;
broken clouds hang low
and high.
Across the valley, sun
burns one blue patch
through the storm's roiling remnants.

III. Shipping

Chicken clucks annoyingly
at doghouse entrance, but
old dog's gone early.
Heifers rumble on
to rickety old scale.
She crouches, ready.
By afternoon, she's
bleeding from her gums,
that stove-up shoulder;
cheekbone flowers bright red too:
calves too fast these days.

Her boy's long gone,
but the work remains to do.
Cloudy eyes tell me her mission:
Stay here. Guard the house.
Help when there are cows to chase.
Die with your boots on.

So go ahead, chicken.
Lay your egg in her yellow nest.
She'll be home tonight,
and appreciate the morsel.

Christmas Bush

Thieves, I hope you read that book you stole.
It won the National Book Award this year.
Use my backpack.
I hope that when you wear my turquoise,
nuggets found in Colorado,
their blue fire burns your skin.
May you have nightmares.
May your girlfriend hate the sweater.
May her throat rash under those silver beads
my husband's gift.
May his work coat,
flannel faded and cowshit-daubed,
not keep you warm.
May you lose sleep over the snapshot
of my father,
small boy and big dog on sand,
"Lordship Beach, 1931."
Feel stupid when you open the big gift:
golf clubs. Come on,
we know you don't play golf.
May someone bash in your teeth
with the titanium-head driver.

May some gentle grace descend on me
and help me find
a vestige of kind spirit
inside all these mean curses.
Bless you, thieves.
may you find solace.
Right after I do.

No cash, no checks,
no credit cards.
No Christmas tree, unless we cut one.
No, he says, no driving all over hell
looking for some juniper;
they make bad Christmas trees anyway.
We compromise.
Sam chops me down a giant sagebrush,
six feet tall.
The gather along this fence line will be easier
next fall.
Knarled trunk,
graceful feathered fronds,
pungent desert evergray.
We plunk it in a feed tub,
nestle tiny red apples and lace angels
between the twigs.
It's just right:
looks nearly dead
but smells so strong.

It's a piece of our life right here,
not some Norwegian woodcutter's Christmas,
nor Christian missionary's coping strategy.

Desert evergreen,
promising redemption
to those who can simply hang on.

Weeks later, a road crew found my wallet in a ditch and returned it to me; the picture of my father and his big dog was intact. I still have it.

Blue Moon New Year's Eve

One joyous hour
skidding in falling snow,
her snow pants wild with butterflies, pink parka smackeroo
of whooping joy skittering on turquoise plastic
down the hill into the feedlot alley,
startling the heifers.
The storm lasts just so long:
time enough for one sledding,
one snowman.

Then it all turns to slush and slop,
muddy boots, frozen pumps:
it's a feed-truck-won't-get-out-of-first-gear-afternoon.

Still, that night,
clouds drift by a big blue moon.
Coyotes howl in joy.
We dig the last of the Chinese fireworks from the back of the closet,
drive out to the highway
so we don't run the horses through the fence.

Her dad's Zippo snaps Whistling Moon Rockets into life,
screaming off into that snow-light desert New Year night.
We pour champagne into metal cups
rattling on the hood.

Poof.
Blue on white on indigo,
red on green,
gold on silver,
tinseling down the darkness.
Silences that coyote chorus;
I'm struck dumb too,
remembering, soaked up
in that moment of silence
after the explosion of something,
where you realize you only just exist
to fill this small space
in this endless midnight world
lit by this giant midnight moon.

On Starting Colts

I.
The days are quiet,
mares gone to winter pasture.
Colts finally settle.

Rake the round corral:
bring blankets, buckets, rope.
Winter's work begins.

Fold and fold again,
slip folds through center knife cut:
soft burlap hobbles.

Unfurl white cotton,
a thousand slender fibers:
braid soft, strong foot rope.

II.
Rain falls on tin roof;
red door creaks open slowly.
Turn colts into barn.

Two paints, a buckskin,
the two wild sorrel stud colts:
this afternoon's class.

Nostrils flaring wide
your every muscle trembling.
Relax and learn, colt.

Voice gentle always,
"Got a kink in your tail there?
Settle down now, Red."

III.
His ears flick forward.
Paint nuzzles for a mouthful,
trusting his teacher.

Dragging halter rope,
permit the brush down your flank,
eat a bite of grain.

IV.
Tidy roan filly:
stubborn, taut, intelligent.
He saves her for last.

"Turn the others out:
it's time to start on Roanie."
Door shuts, light lowers.

Loop sails over neck.
She won't be like the others.
Up, up she rises.

Hobble front and hind.
Your squealing will not help you:
learn to stand, filly.

Quick as lightning's bolt
hind feet flash toward you.
"Did she get you, Dad?"

"She didn't hurt me."
Turn away a moment, on
next day's purple shins.

Patience, patience now.
There is no place for anger
in a good teacher.

Supple willow wand
drags crusty burlap over
trembling roan haunches.

V.
At last, she trusts him,
stands quivering in hobbles.
Adrenalin fades.

Don't lay your ears back!
It's time to go to water.
Step out lightly, girl.

She leads easy now.
This season's work is finished.
Until springtime, then.

Colt-Starting Diplomacy

That sorrel paint was hot,
thinking about striking.
The old man leaned
his big scarred fists
against the young stud's chest—
just met the pressure;
he wasn't pushing back.
The colt tried him three times,
shoving up against him.
Then, flicking his ears, he breathed.
Not calm yet, but not mad either,
the old man all the time
talking to him
softly.

Heart of Winter

I split four pumpkins yesterday
as the snow fell,
the old doe boldly stepping up to paw
sweet meat inside the rind.
Someone's haystack is on fire up the valley,
a tower of flame in the cracking cold.
Blue-white barchan dunes of snow
left from last night's windstorm
reflect the dying orange of breathless evening
as she feasts one more time before night falls.

January, Montana

"We'll sell every old cow we have,"
the grizzled rancher says,
his face tired with fighting
the weather, the bureaucrats, the acts of God
that seem to come just when you need a break.
"Miles of fence are gone."

I shake my head,
cross my fingers,
keep looking for pasture
like everybody else. Fifteen months later
the trucks pull out to the sale yard,
three decades of family history aboard.
We're not done yet, but
it's tough to be jolly
when the wolves are at the door.

Pogonip

Ice crystals drift inches deep
in paths we shoveled yesterday.
At night they fling themselves against the glass,
tick-tick-ticking
the tale of their Arctic journey,
arrowing from the Pole
to cover my trees, my cats
my quail.

They rest there,
frozen death blanket,
for days, weeks,
eight inches thick
grown a crushing weight.

Power poles snap like toothpicks
over the pass;
wires snake across the road
tangling in the frozen sage.

We growl at each other
across the kitchen table.

No stars in the black night
for six weeks now.

At Last, One Night

The killing fog slinks away,
dragging its deadly lacework blanket.
Desert stars on a cloak of midnight,
remind us of our place in the universe.

In next dawn's blush on frozen hill,
dogs, horses, everything stills
to watch the great red orb break the horizon:

in a moment, the greatest gift.
Yes, let there be

light.

Valentine's Day

Darkening dusk of a Friday afternoon,
cowboy knocks at the door,
defeat on his face.
Slapping bloody gloves, he says
"Heifer's too small, calf's too big."
We load her up, head for town.

Freezing rain whips in the gathering dark.
Hat tilted against the wind,
he unhooks the gooseneck
behind the concrete operating room.
"You might as well go get groceries," he says.
"This is going to take awhile."

I buy milk, bread, canned tomatoes.
I take my time in the hardware store,
staring at paint.
I was going to fix the place up
last week
for our anniversary.

At seven p.m. I push through the door
into the bright-white space.
Red heifer's still standing.
Long dark hair and girlish smile,
the vet wipes her face on her sleeve,
pools of blood at her feet.

Steel chute holds the patient tight,
so she doesn't kick the doctor.
"Hold this suture for me?"
I sit on the stool next to her, watch
strong quick hands twist the curved needle,
long fingers catch a cat's cradle of tissue:
spin, twist, tie; spin, twist, tie
through the tough hide.
"I'm getting slower," she shakes her head.
"Tired."
Both of us cut sutures, helping her finish.
She might as well have her Friday night.

I don't ask about the calf.

The weather's no better on the way out.
Home late,
we park the trailer
out in front,
leave that heifer in it overnight.
We eat sandwiches I picked up in town,
watch TV without talking
for our anniversary dinner.

Waiting for the Right Wind

She's getting some age on her,
he said,
as though it were a patina,
old paint
that might be peeled, scraped,
buffed away.
Like the rings of trees,
growing a carapace thicker each year
better able to withstand the winds of winter
until, with agonizing slowness,
the heartwood rots
and one day the whole trunk cracks in half.

How long do we stand,
dead inside,
appearing to be among the lively,
when we are really just waiting
for the right wind
to bring us to rest?

Safe Harbor

The night's dark blanket
cannot smother my dreaming,
longing for your smile.

Tiny sleeping girl-child
dreams hot, welded to my side,
fills my heart's chasm.

Months pass, years.
Drifting away.
Grandmother stares into midnight's void:
Calling you, calling.

Winter Haiku

Through dense flakes falling
rifle sight fogs with moisture.
Cannot get a shot.

Heifer's young carcass
tunneled now by ruthless fangs:
black hide under snow.

We count four, five, six
shaggy coyotes gorging on
young mother's flesh.

Seven shadows ghost
through moon-bright silent meadow
bringing death swiftly.

Taking Refuge

Coyotes drive them out
of winter meadow, to sleep
in porch light's circle.

Winter miracle:
a four-point buck greets morning
on my frozen lawn.

Great brown eyes meet mine
over my first steaming cup
of morning java.

The feast of apples,
grapes left just outside the fence:
princesses, they graze.

CHAPTER 5
OVER THE YEARS

Cairn: Woman Sculpted of Stones

She crouches there
in autumn sunshine,
human form outlined in steel.
Grandmother, filled with stones,
held back by structure
from the angle of repose.

White quartz cobbles,
pieces of the earth
tumbled down canyon river:
gathered fragments of our mother.

So feminine to remain,
to permit abrasion
beneath running water's surface,
to be made smooth.
Not soft.

Quartz is nearly hard as diamond
in the mineral scheme of things,
yet beneath the weight of mountains,
quartz flows.
The stones are individuals at first glance
but closer scrutiny reveals another truth.

Bonded rows of atoms
as though locking arms, shift as one:
Translation, it's called.

Boundaries between grains
press inexorably together
so tightly we name them sutures.

And so, we are sutured
by the weight of mountains,
the press of experience,
metamorphosed
into each other,
translated into another,
harder version of ourselves.
Welded, smoothed, female.
Sustained heavy pressure: in the end
it makes us stronger.

As with quartz pebbles,
only the sudden sharp strike causes us
to shatter,
to fall into a handful
of unrecognizable fragments.
It is the speed of the blow
that scatters us,
each shard
to be smoothed in its turn:
the seeds of our daughters.

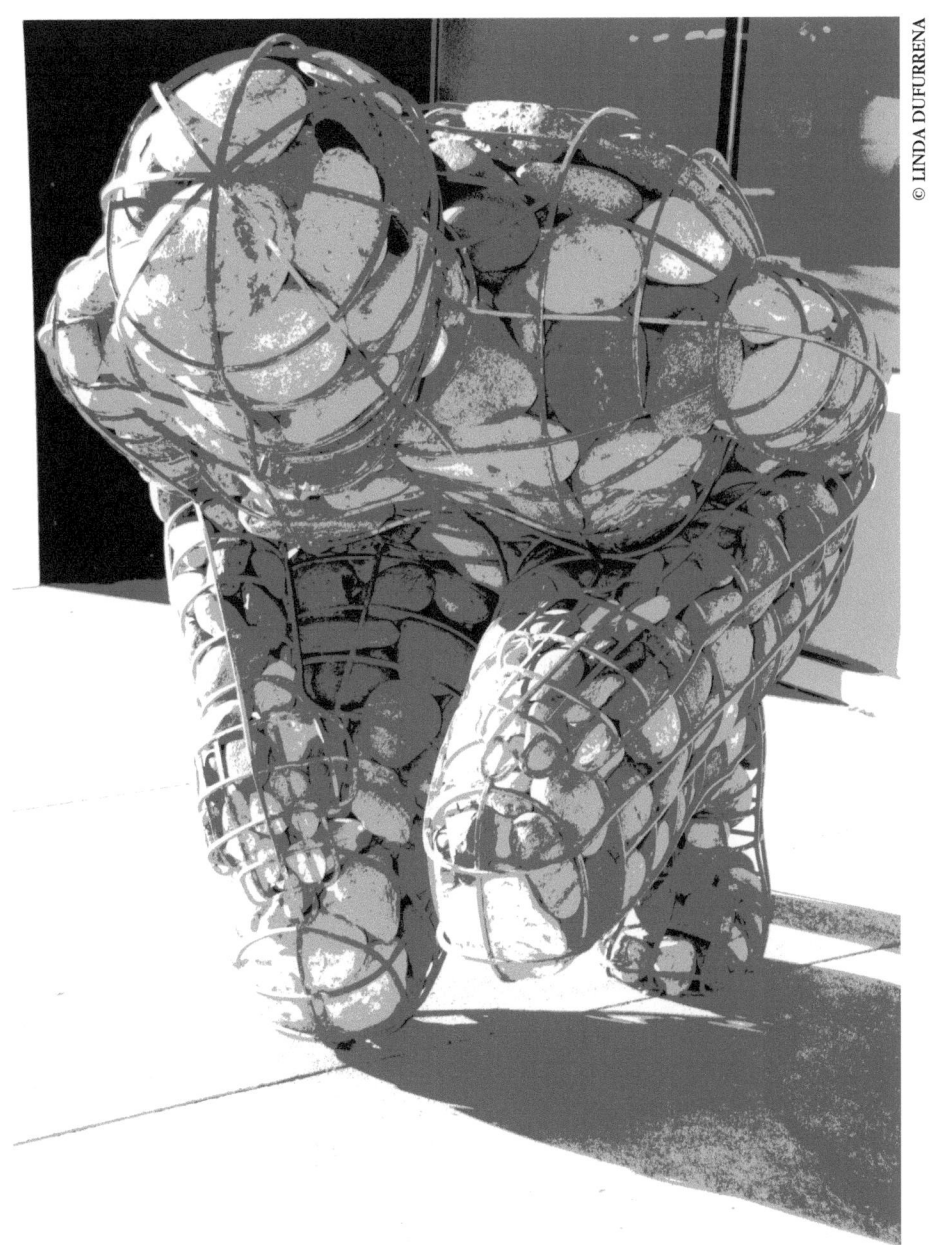

Buster's Horses

Perhaps his first horse was a dog, at least one likes to think so, a burly long-haired border collie, or a rangy Catahoula, that he could curl his small two-year-old fists into, and ride around the yard beneath the cherry trees.

The next mount a gentle mule: by the age of five, he was on his way to sheep camp up the canyon with his cousin, to while away the afternoons with the camp tender, fishing in the little creek and following along as the old Basque made his circle through the sheep camps scattered across the ridges.

Soon old enough to ride the seven miles down to school in the little desert town, he'd stable his steady horse in the old rock barn across the road, and then ride home after class. When the weather got bad and the days were short they'd drive him; his father would make a free hour to get him down to town.

A buckaroo horse was next, to carry him, so young still, on a man's work day, across the valley, around the point to the hay meadows twenty miles distant, following the steers to summer pasture. Carry him home, back across the long valleys all the long way that afternoon, stopping in the town with his older brother, sleeping on a chair in the bar while listening to the talk of war. Riding the rest of the way in the dark, back to the ranch, under the stars.

Then the wild buckers and mustangs of young manhood, horses hard to ride, with unexpected fits and starts that would throw a guy headfirst into a greasewood, horses they didn't start till they were five years old. The horses were ready for the tough work they'd have to do, but you'd better be ready, too, they said. He was part of a crew of young men those years, brothers all. They rode everything, and proved everything they needed to prove.

Later on, with work to do, he rode a tall strong long-walking horse, one that could outwalk a lesser beast trotting alongside. They'd ride out before daylight, go all day through the rocks, brand when they got there, and walk the long miles home, resting those horses, day after day. They were tough horses, tough men to ride them. Years of that, riding for the work he loved.

Later still, there was less time spent horseback and more in the truck, as the demands of the ranch increased. It was then he gathered up mares to raise the colts, that would grow into the kind of horses he envisioned, strong enough to carry a man all day, and gentle enough to carry his grandkids. That's what he was after.

His last horse was a swather. He rode it with his big border collie alongside in the cab. The dog kept him awake, kept him company the long hours. He rode up and down the meadows and alfalfa fields, his dog in the cab, his grandson in the swather beside him, still trying to keep up, the old man not hurrying but going steady, steady, for hours and hours. He'd stop for lunch, but the kid would skip the meal, or eat in his machine so he could catch up. In the last years, the old man would stop sometimes at the end of a windrow, just for a few minutes, and have a little nap. The dog would snuffle at his hand, lick his face, reminding him that it was time to rouse himself, get going again.

Homeland Security: For Miguel

March

They say the river will run soon.
Snow is heavy in the high country: time
for Miguel to go to work.

For years, the men sharpened their shovels
in the fall,
the day before they left.
In spring, they would return,
or their brothers or cousins in their place,
each knowing where the shovel waited,
in the corner of the shop.
Sling familiar, sharpened tool onto shoulder,
head out into the fields.

The meadows need Miguel.
They remember each other.

July

Breeze blows across the meadow
deep in rye grass, bluestem, fescue.
An ocean of softness bending
to the wind's touch
across all things standing still.
The waving grass conceals his journey
across the field
as he changes water,
the tiny figure wading to his shoulders
in meadow hay.

He surfaces,
the flash of his shovel blade
like a fish jumping
in a green sea.

December

Icy wind cuts to the bone.
I hurry to the woodshed
through the freezing afternoon.

Three rows deep, firewood packed
thoughtfully: not too heavy, nor
too high for me,
stacked on a crisp and golden
October afternoon.

Miguel's axe still echoes
from that autumn twilight
that slides slowly into evening.
Hours after his work day finished,
he split the head-high pile of rounds
against this day.

An aging man's last gift to me
before he left for winter,
to warm up, see his wife, and this time,
come back legal.

Miguel's gift warms me now
in winter's heart
as he waits in Hermosillo, hungry;
his wife, waiting in Colima, hungry
for the visa that will not come,
not this winter, not next spring, not ever.

A simple, honest man,
he has told them yes, one time,
he came to America without papers.
No visa. Not now, not ever.

Homeland security.
He was part of ours.

Chief

He came with the saddle string, when the ranch sold. The new owner said,
"He's lame. Can't ride him? Sell him."
Long-legged sorrel, runnin' red Appaloosa;
the tattoo in his lip told the story of his youth.
"He'll do anything you ask him to, the old bastard," Tim said.
"Go all day. If you kick him in the belly, you better be ready to hang on."

He'd been there a while when we got the job.
They called him Winduri, Spanish for leopard,
and that was how he moved, stretched out and sleek.
Tim was the cowboss, and he took him from the Mexicans, put him in his string.
They were a pair, those two,
with the same go-all-day-through-the-rocks-
and-brand-when-you-get-there sense of the world.
Twelve hours gathering, Chief trotted sideways down the canyon all the way home.
Ten years or so, they were the perfect match
when they went to run burros on the refuge.

Burros are smart, hard to catch. Nine cowboys and a helicopter
ran flat out all day.
One burro too many. A center crack, just a hairline,
opened on that right front foot.
He shod it, laid him off awhile, but it never quite closed.
Still they worked, tiny fractures in man and horse
snaking through their bones.
Not many things hurt so bad you can't work.
The ranch changed hands again, and two years now he's ranged the pasture,
lame or not so lame.
Can't take him on the mountain any more.

Finally the new guy says, "Take him to the sale."
All the cowboss says is, "Well,
one day he'll have to take that mare he's so in love with,
and that'll be a different story."

A lot of horses, you can just sell 'em.
But not all horses.
"Find a place for him if you can," he says.

"So there's this teacher gal in town," I say.
"She rides a little."
Got a broken leg and no trailer,
a big brushy corral on the hillside,
an obnoxious pinto gelding.

He cracks the hint of a smile.
"Damn pony'll learn some manners."

The gray morning dawns, the trailer pulls out.
He comes home lighter than I've seen him in while.
"Those folks are clueless,
but they've got a pile of hay.
It's sandy ground, there's a little trail right there.
She said they'd take it easy.
If they feed him, he'll be fine.
Hell, he's better off.
Better off than going to the sale."

Wanted to Trade

Wanted to trade: your ride for mine.
My ride: old silver Caddy, long, low and lean;
hydraulic levelers, wire wheels—
shoot, they're five hundred dollars apiece.
Lots of miles, but she's been well cared for.

Your ride: one good horse,
knows what a cow is;
tall strong and straight,
something with a future:
something your wife could ride.

My ride's a smooth one,
but it's time for something else.
Two steady mounts are crippled for good;
five thousand bucks isn't easy to come by,
and nobody I know with a good horse
takes Mastercard.

A good cow horse, for me this time.
Our son darn near grown, the next
ten years in the house
loom before me like a dark shadow.
It's either drive somewhere
or get something to drive cows with.

Twenty-five hundred,
that's a good investment
on the next ten years,
before my husband
climbs down for good,
before his body
makes him quit.
(I see you lean on the gate post,
look at the trees,
take a breath
before you walk down the path,
stove up again.)

Shoeing horses,
I watch the span of your back,
bent under the balancing
of the big sorrel's haunch.
Horseflies are bad,
the gelding shivers and fidgets.
I think of the x-rays, tiny s-curves:
lightning bolts
down your lumbar vertebrae.
Got you off the hay crew anyway.
It's an ill wind, they say,
blows no good.

Twenty-five hundred dollars,
sounds like a lot,
but think of the best days
of our life together:
most of them have been horseback.
Cold, hot, rainy, snow
blowing in my face
the day we brought the leppie calf back,
riding blind,
breathing in pellets of driving snow,
trusting that palomino horse
to know the way home.
That calf made it too.

Another day,
topping the highest ridge
anywhere around
just at daybreak,
folds of hills and canyons blushing red,
You turned around and pointed:
three buck deer,
antlers like tree branches
lounging on the basalt ledge.
Show me the things nobody sees but you.
Keep showing me.
I'll get myself a new ride.

Mapping the Landscape of the Heart

The cold desert toughens the heart. Harshness of drought, snow without moisture, and the relentless heat of summer build a carapace that allows tenderness to survive within. The heart's meadows open with the gift of rain on sagebrush, with a January sunset that lights the monochromatic landscape.

Elizabeth, spare and taut of spirit, comes to the desert during the Depression. She has only this choice: to coax potatoes and onions from the clay, or starve. She digs a trench four inches deep in alkali. Rocks divert the flow and guide the paltry stream into the next row when the ditch fills just so far. She nurtures tiny plants on the waterline.

Her companions are the wild creatures. She opens the back door on summer evenings, when the breeze down the canyon cools her breathless kitchen, so that a giant bullsnake can slide in. He coils on the concrete floor under the refrigerator. She defends his presence: "We don't have any problem with mice." The creatures give her a measure of joy and allow her to continue scrabbling in the tight soil, confident in another year's crop of mouse-free spuds.

We are kinder in the wet years, more

generous, as though the earth's gifts soak our parched souls. In a year lush with fruit, the old cut-eared doe comes into the yard to find tubs of gathered apples spread across the gravel; next day she brings compatriots. Neighbors drive by, see the gathering. The day after, more apples arrive from ranches up the valley. There is a generosity of spirit: share when there is plenty.

Wild fluctuations in the natural world imprint themselves on our hearts: the harshness of fire and flood, the austere beauty of rugged terrain, the distant, aching sweetness of a desert sunrise are the forces that shape the landscape of the heart.

There are no signposts to help us map this inner landscape. Home lies at the edge of the map, where the first surveyors stood looking at the desert and said, this is far enough. Yet this is where the greatest secrets lie, in the solitude of the desert wind, at the edge of experience, the landscape at the edge of the map.

Miguel: Afterword

Miguel called, the old man said.
He's back in California.
He frowned. Don't have anything right now.
But surely in the spring? Did he leave a phone number?
A way to get in touch?
No. Of course not.
He is floating in the world,
in the cities of California,
a man meant to live
in the country, in the fields,
with the water.
Maybe, next spring,
the rains will blow him up this way.
Maybe when snow is melting in the mountains,
that will remind him of his shovel,
waiting in the shop.
He will bravely call again,
remember the fields, and the water,
and maybe then
he will come back to us.